An Earwig in the Ear

Nigel Gray

Stanley Thornes (Publishers) Ltd

Contents

Originally published in 1979 by Hutchinson Education
Reprinted 1980, 1981, 1982, 1983, 1985, 1987, 1989

Reprinted in 1990 by
Stanley Thornes (Publishers) Ltd
Old Station Drive
Leckhampton
CHELTENHAM GL53 0DN

British Library Cataloguing in Publication Data

Gray, N
An earwig in the ear.
—(Spirals series; 1).
1. Readers — Drama
I. Title II. Series
428.6'2 PE1121

ISBN 0 7487 0367 5

Cover illustration by Simon Rees, cover design by Ned Hoste

Set in IBM Pyramid
Printed and bound in Great Britain by
Martin's of Berwick

An Earwig in the Ear

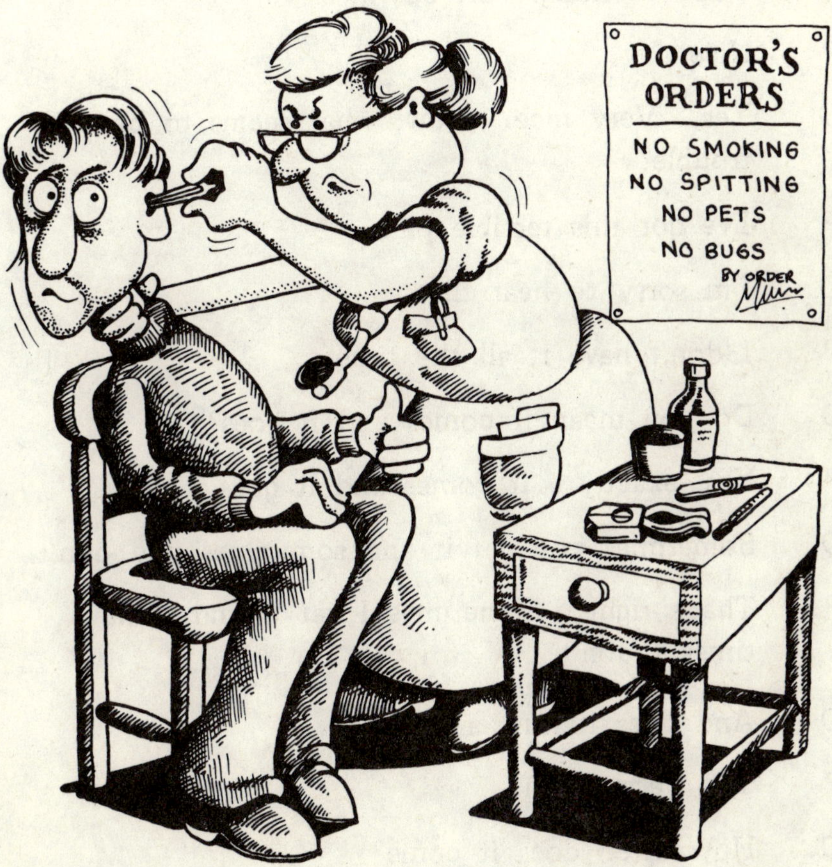

An Earwig in the Ear

Scene: A Doctor's surgery. A *Person* enters to see the *Doctor*.

D Come in.

P Good morning, Doctor.

D Good morning. Sit down.

P Nice day.

D Yes. Very nice. Now, what seems to be the trouble?

P I've got this terrible pain.

D I'm sorry to hear that.

P I don't have it all the time.

D Do you mean it comes and it goes?

P Yes, exactly. It comes and it goes.

D Sometimes you get it and sometimes you don't.

P That's right. Sometimes I get it and sometimes I don't.

D And does it hurt a lot?

P Yes, very much.

D How often does it come?

P That's the worst thing about it.

D What is?

P Well, you never know when it's going to strike.

D You mean it might come at any moment.

P Yes. I might be sitting drinking a cup of tea, as right as rain. And then it comes.

D Just like that.

P Just like that. One minute I'm sitting on my chair. The next minute I'm rolling on the floor.

D May I ask why you roll on the floor?

P Because the pain is so bad.

D Does rolling on the floor get rid of the pain?

P No.

D Then why do you roll on the floor?

P I can't help it.

D Does the pain have any other effects?

P Yes. It makes me jump in the air.

D You roll on the floor, *and* jump in the air.

P Yes. And I bang my head on the wall.

D Anything else?

P I tear my hair out.

D Yes, as soon as you came in I saw you were going bald.

P And I scream terrible blood-curdling screams.

D You roll on the floor, jump in the air, bang your head on the wall, tear your hair out and scream.

P Yes.

D And then what happens?

P The people next door call the police.

D Why do the people next door call the police?

P They think someone is trying to kill me.

D What do they do when they find no one is trying to kill you?

P They try to kill me.

D Have you found anything that helps with the pain?

P No. Nothing.

D You still haven't told me where the pain is.

P I beg your pardon?

D Where is the pain?

P Ear.

D	Where?
P	Ear.
D	Have you got a sore ear?
P	No. I haven't got a saw here. What do you want a saw for? Are you going to cut my ear off?
D	Of course not. I asked if you had a *sore ear.*
P	I thought you asked if I had a *saw here.*
D	Not at all. Can you tell me when the pains in your ear started?
P	It was after I'd been camping.
D	Perhaps you got a chill in it.
P	No, no. It wasn't a chill.
D	How do you know?
P	Because it was an earwig.
D	How do you know it was an earwig?
P	My friend saw it crawl in.
D	What did your friend do when he saw it crawl in?
P	He ran out of the tent, screaming.
D	Oh.

P But by then it was too late.

D You mean, the earwig had gone right in.

P Yes indeed.

D Well, I think the best thing would be for me to try to pull the little fellow out.

P Will it hurt?

D No. It won't hurt. Not very much. Please lie on the bed.

P Shall I get undressed?

D There's no need. Just close your eyes.

P Can you see anything?

D It's like looking into a coal mine.

P Are you trying to say my ears are dirty?

D I can't see. It's too dark in there.

P Shall I turn my head to the light?

D Yes. That's better. Now, what's this?

P Can you see the earwig?

D No. All I can see is a bent hair-pin.

P I tried to get the earwig out with that.

D Well, keep still. I've got to dig deeper.

P Ow, ow! That hurt. Have you got it?

D No, that was a lump of wax and a ball of cotton wool.

P I can't stand much more of this. Hurry up.

D I think I've got it. Yes, yes . . . no, it's just a button.

P That's the button off my cuff. I looked all over the place for that.

D If you don't stop talking I'll never find the earwig. Your ear flaps up and down when you talk.

P Sorry. Ow, ow! It's hurting. I'll have to roll on the floor, jump in the air, bang my head. . . .

D Please, please. Don't start all that.

P I'm doing my best. I'm trying.

D Yes, you're very trying. I'm afraid I must sit on your chest.

P It hurts. It hurts.

D It's nearly over now.

P Have you got him?

D I've got his tail with my tweezers. But he's hanging on like grim death.

P Help!

D Here he comes.

P He's pulling my ear inside out.

D He's hanging on. But I'm winning.

P I can't bear it any more.

D Keep still, I don't want to hurt the poor little fellow. Here he comes now. Got him.

P You mean he's out?

D Yes. Just look at him.

P No more pain.

D Isn't he lovely? You can tell he's glad to be out.

P No more rolling on the floor.

D What lovely markings. I'm very interested in insects, you know.

P No more jumping in the air.

D I'll take this one home, and put him in my collection.

P No more banging my head on the wall, and pulling my hair out.

D Look at his little legs. Isn't he lovely?

P No more screaming those blood-curdling screams.

D And what a pretty tail.

P I'll never go camping again.

D Oh. Oh dear.

P What's the matter?

D I think you'd better come back next week.

P Why? What for?

D I'm afraid it isn't a little fellow after all.

P What do you mean?

D It's a little lady.

P So what?

D And I'm afraid she's just laid her eggs. In your ear.

P Oh no!

D Please. Please. Stop rolling on the floor like that.

Grannie's Holiday

Grannie's Holiday

Scene: A police station. Two characters. A *Person* comes in to see the police *Officer.*

P Excuse me.

O Good afternoon.

P I've got something to report.

O What sort of something?

P Well, I'm not sure.

O What do you mean?

P Well, it might be a missing person.

O Might be?

P Yes. Or then again, it might be theft.

O But surely it must be one or the other.

P Or on the other hand, it might be both.

O Both?

P Yes. Or then again, it might be something quite different.

O What ever do you mean?

P Well, you see, I've come to report a death.

O I think you'd better start at the beginning and tell me the whole story.

P Yes. Of course. You see, I was on holiday.

O You *were* on holiday.

P Well, that is, I *am* on holiday.

O On your own?

P No, no. I've got my two children with me. And my mother.

O You've got two children with you, and your mother.

P Well no. Not exactly.

O But you just said. . . .

P Yes, yes. True. I did.

O Well what do you mean?

P What do I mean?

O Yes. What exactly do you mean?

P Well, that's what I'm trying to tell you.

O First you say you've got two children and your mother with you. And then you say, not exactly.

P Well, perhaps I should have said I *had* them with me.

O *Had?*

P Yes, had.

O You've come to report that your children are missing.

P Oh, no. No.

O But you said, you *had* them with you.

P Yes, that's true.

O But you haven't got them with you any more.

P Oh, yes. Yes, I have.

O Where are they now?

P They're here.

O Where's here?

P They're just sitting outside.

O You're sure?

P Oh, yes. I'm sure.

O You're sure you're sure?

P Oh, yes. I just left them sitting out there a minute ago.

O Then you could say that you *have* got your children with you.

P Oh, yes. Indeed I could.

O Then why did you say that you *had* them with you?

P Well I did have them with me *as well?*

O What on earth are you talking about?

P I'm trying to explain.

O Well, come to the point then.

P Yes, of course. You see, I had my children with me, *and* my mother.

O And now you've got your children with you?

P Yes. That's right.

O And your mother?

P Well, it's Grannie that's the problem, you see.

O Where is your grannie?

P No, no. She's not *my* grannie. She's the children's grannie. We all just call her Grannie.

O Very well. Where is Grannie?

P Ah.

O Ah, what?

P That's just it.

O Well, where *is* Grannie?

P I don't know.

O I see.

P That's what I came to see you about.

O You mean that Grannie's gone wandering off somewhere. Well, we'll soon find her. Don't worry.

P I'm afraid it's not as simple as that.

O Why not?

P Grannie's dead.

O Dead?

P Yes. She died this morning.

O God rest her soul.

P We were on a camping holiday. In fact, we *are* on a camping holiday.

O And Grannie was camping with you?

P Yes. Up till yesterday she was fit as a fiddle.

O Then what happened?

P We all got up this morning. Except Grannie.

O Grannie stayed in bed?

P She passed away in the night.

O Is she still in the tent?

P No.

O Well where is she?

P I'm coming to that.

O I wish you would.

P Well, you see, I didn't know what to do. With Grannie being dead.

O It's a difficult situation.

P So I wrapped her up in her sleeping bag. Then I put her in the car.

O And is she still in the car?

P I don't know.

O What do you mean, you don't know?

P Well, I'm not sure. At least, I'm pretty sure she's not *in* the car.

O What on earth are you talking about?

P Well, as you know, it's been a very hot day.

O What's that got to do with it?

P The children started to complain about the smell.

O What smell?

P The smell of Grannie in the car.

O So what did you do?

P I took Grannie out of the car.

O And where did you put her?

P On the roof rack.

O So Grannie's on the roof rack of your car.

P I'm not sure.

O Why aren't you sure?

P Well, the children were hungry.

O For goodness sake. You're not going to tell me they've eaten Grannie?

P No, no. Oh dear me, no. Nothing like that.

O Well what happened?

P I stopped at a café.

O Did you enjoy your meal?

P The chips were a bit soggy.

O I'm sorry to hear that.

P When we finished our meal, we came out of the café.

O Having paid your bill.

P Of course.

O And then?

P Ah.

O Ah, what?

P That's the problem.

O What is the problem, exactly?

P Someone has stolen our car.

Lunch Break

Lunch Break

Scene: The Directors' dining room of a large company. Two characters. A *Worker* enters and sits at a table beside a *Director*.

W Hello.

D I'm afraid you can't sit there.

W Why not? There's plenty of room.

D I beg your pardon?

W You've got plenty of room. In the works canteen it's much more crowded.

D Look, you ought not to be here.

W Your dinner looks good. I think I'll have the same.

D I said you're in the wrong place. Only directors can eat here.

W I don't see why. This feels just the place for me.

D Really! This is a bit much! You should be in the works canteen.

W But it's much nicer here.

D I'll have you thrown out.

W What about those men there? You haven't told them to get out.

D They are directors.

W Well, are their stomachs different from mine?

D That's not the point.

W Yes, it is the point. Why should they eat a different lunch from me?

D You don't seem to understand.

W I do understand. Every human body lives on the same food.

D Of course. No one is denying that.

W Then why can't I eat here with these others?

D Well, for one thing, you can't afford the food here.

W How much does it cost then?

D Well, in fact, this food is not for sale.

W You mean that these directors don't have to pay for their food?

D Their meals are provided by the company.

W But that's not fair.

D Why not?

W They can afford to pay more because they earn more – but they get their meals free.

D Well, they are directors.

W But why do we workers have to pay for our food in the works canteen when we earn less?

D I don't wish to talk about it now.

W When will you talk about it, then?

D I don't wish to talk about it at all.

W Why did you say that I couldn't afford it if the meals are free?

D Because I want you to leave at once.

W But I haven't had anything to eat yet.

D You've got your own canteen to go to.

W But it's not as nice as this one.

D This firm has one canteen fit for workers and another fit for directors.

W Well, why is one canteen so much nicer than the other?

D Because the directors need a quiet place, to help the food go down.

W And what about the workers? They get rotten food. Don't they need a quiet place to help it go down?

D I don't know about that. But I do know that you should not be here.

W But I'd like to have a good meal for a change.

D You can get a good meal in your own canteen.

W Well, why don't you go to the works canteen today in my place and have a good meal, and I'll have my meal here in your place.

D Certainly not.

W Why not?

D Because I don't want to. And I don't understand what you're doing here in the first place.

W I told you. I came to get a meal.

D I have been with this firm for more than twenty years, and this is the first time one of the workers has come in here.

W Well, someone must make a start some time.

D I'm asking you to leave. Please.

W All right. I've got nothing against you.

D Then for my sake. Will you please go?

W Yes. Yes, I will.

D Thank you.

W Just as soon as I've had my dinner.

D But you can't have your dinner here.

W I'll be late back to work if I don't eat here now. You've wasted so much of my time already.

D Have you been drinking this morning?

W No. I'm stone cold sober.

D Are you sure?

W Peter Piper picked a peck of pickled pepper.

D I beg your pardon?

W Peter Piper picked a peck of pickled pepper.

D I do believe you *are* drunk.

W I'm not. You try saying that.

D You could be sacked for being drunk.

W But I tell you I'm not drunk.

D You know very well that it is forbidden to drink while you are at work.

W What about those directors? They are all drinking wine.

D That's got nothing to do with it.

W Will they be sacked?

D No, they won't. A drink at lunch-time helps the directors to relax. Then they work better.

W Well, wouldn't it help *us* work better?

D No. You are a worker with this firm. Not a director. And this is not the way for a worker to carry on.

W Well, I don't see why it shouldn't be the same for me as for them.

D Look, you must go. The directors have all sorts of important things to talk about.

W Well, I'm not stopping them.

D They can't talk with you here. These things are private.

W Private?

D Yes, private. Secret.

W But I'm sure they've got nothing to hide.

D Of course they've got nothing to hide.

W So why should they mind me hearing what they have to say?

D You wouldn't understand what they're talking about.

W Then why would it matter if I overheard them?

D Listen. That seat you are sitting on is not yours. Someone else will need it.

W Where is he?

D He's coming soon.

W I'll get up when he comes.

D He'll be here shortly.

W That's all right. When he comes I'll move to another seat.

D But all these seats will be needed.

W I'm hungry. Do you have to wait all this time for your food?

D I simply can't understand why you have come in here at all.

W One reason is that my doctor told me I mustn't eat the sort of fatty food that we get in the works canteen.

D But that doesn't mean to say that you should come in here.

W Oh yes. Because the food that is served in here is much better for me.

D Look. Everyone in this firm has his own workplace.

W I know that.

D Well, you can't just sit down at someone else's workplace and do that person's work, can you?

W That's not the same. It takes time to learn a job. But anyone can eat.

D Well, I can't eat if I'm sitting next to someone like you.

W You should be pleased that someone like me comes to visit you sometimes.

D Look. You have your place, and I have mine. If you don't like it you can get another job. It's up to you. That's fair, isn't it?

W It's hard to find a job at the moment, and I think I'd like to be a director. You'll be leaving any day now, won't you? I can see you are well past 65. Maybe I can have your job.

D I've only got one more thing to say to you.

W What's that?

D You're fired.

A complete list of Spirals

Stories

Jim Alderson
Crash in the Jungle
The Witch Princess

Jan Carew
Death Comes to the Circus

Susan Duberley
The Ring

Keith Fletcher and Susan Duberley
Nightmare Lake

John Goodwin
Dead-end Job

Paul Groves
Not that I'm Work-shy
The Third Climber

Anita Jackson
The Actor
The Austin Seven
Bennet Manor
Dreams
The Ear
A Game of Life or Death
No Rent to Pay

Paul Jennings
Eye of Evil
Maggot

Margaret Loxton
The Dark Shadow

Patrick Nobes
Ghost Writer

Kevin Philbin
Summer of the Werewolf

John Townsend
Beware of the Morris Minor
Fame and Fortune
SOS

David Walke
Dollars in the Dust

Plays

Jan Carew
Computer Killer
No Entry
Time Loop

John Godfrey
When I Count to Three

Nigel Gray
An Earwig in the Ear

Paul Groves
Tell Me Where it Hurts

Barbara Mitchelhill
Punchlines
The Ramsbottoms at Home

Madeline Sotherby
Hard Times at Batwing Hall

John Townsend
Cheer and Groan
The End of the Line
Hanging by a Fred
The Lighthouse Keeper's Secret
Making a Splash
Murder at Muckleby Manor
Over and Out
Taking the Plunge

David Walke
The Bungle Gang Strikes Again
The Good, the Bad and the Bungle
Package Holiday